Audrey Hepburn

CHRIS RICE

Level 2

Series Editors: Andy Hopkins and Jocelyn Potter

Pearson Education Limited
Edinburgh Gate, Harlow,
Essex CM20 2JE, England
and Associated Companies throughout the world.

ISBN: 978-1-4058-7698-8

First published by Penguin Books 2000
This edition first published by Pearson Education 2008

5 7 9 10 8 6 4

Typeset by Graphicraft Ltd, Hong Kong
Set in 11/14pt Bembo
Printed in China
SWTC/04

Published by Pearson Education Ltd in association with
Penguin Books Ltd, a Penguin Random House company.

Acknowledgments:
Aquarius Library: pp. 1, 5, and 17; BFI: pp. 7, 11, 15, and 22;
The Kobal Collection: pp. 9 and 10; The Ronald Grant Archive: pp. 13 and 19;
Rex Features: p. 20

Every effort has been made to trace copyright holders in every case.

For a complete list of the titles available in the Penguin Readers series please write to your local
Pearson Longman office or to: Penguin Readers Marketing Department, Pearson Education,
Edinburgh Gate, Harlow, Essex CM20 2JE, England.

Contents

Introduction

Audrey worked hard at her dancing. She had no time for boyfriends. One day the ballet school told her: "I'm sorry, but you'll never be a famous dancer. You're too tall."

Audrey was sad, but then something happened. It changed her life . . .

And it changed the lives of millions of other people, too. She made about thirty movies and became one of the most famous people in the world.

Audrey Hepburn was a ballet dancer, but she never danced in a ballet. She made more money than any other movie actress, but she never studied acting. There was something different about her. A friend said, "In some ways, Audrey Hepburn is the same as other young girls. But in other ways, she is different from them all." In *Breakfast at Tiffany's*, Audrey sits at a window and sings a beautiful sad song. When she sings that song, suddenly she is not an actress. People think that they know her. They think she is their friend.

The world loved her. People love her now, years after she died. But she was not always happy. There were sad times when she was a child. Some famous people did not like her. Behind a lot of her greatest movies, there are some unhappy stories. She had many problems, but she always showed a warm face to the world. And behind that face, there really was a nice, warm person.

In this book you will learn many interesting things about Audrey Hepburn. Why did the daughter of a baroness have to dig vegetables from the ground for food? Why did the famous movie director, Alfred Hitchcock, not like her? Why did the world's most successful actress stop making movies when she was only forty-five years old?

This is not only the story of a famous actress. It is also the story of a wonderful person.

Chapter 1   Music is for Dancing

One day, in a big house in Brussels, Belgium, a man took his daughter in his arms. Little Audrey Hepburn looked up and saw some beautiful lights above her. They were as white as snow. She remembered those lights all her life. She always loved the color white. She saw white and remembered her father. Then she felt safe and warm.

Audrey Kathleen van Heemstra Hepburn-Ruston was born in Brussels on May 4, 1929. Her mother, Baroness Ella van Heemstra, was Dutch. Her father, Joseph, was half English, half Irish. He worked for many companies and made a lot of money.

Young Audrey enjoyed reading and loved animals and birds. But her greatest love was music. "What's music?" Audrey asked

Audrey with her mother, Baroness Ella van Heemstra.

her mother one day. "It's for dancing," her mother answered.

Audrey wanted to be a dancer, but she was unhappy. "I'm too fat," she thought. "Dancers are thin and pretty, but my face is too round and my legs are too big."

Her parents were unhappy too. They often fought. One night her mother and father had a big fight. When Audrey woke up the next morning, her father was not there. Audrey cried for days.

Her mother took her to England. At school, Audrey was different from the other girls. The other girls were funny and noisy. They enjoyed sports and talked about their fathers. Audrey was quiet and sad. Her English was not good and she hated sports. She did not talk to anybody about her father. But, slowly, Audrey began to make some friends.

Then suddenly, in 1939, her mother took her away from England. She could not say goodbye to her schoolfriends. There was no time. "Why are we leaving?" Audrey asked.

"There's going to be a war," her mother told her. "We're going to Holland. You'll be safe there."

Audrey lived with her mother and two half-brothers in the Dutch town of Arnhem. She became more and more interested in dancing. At the age of ten she wanted to be a world-famous ballet dancer. But one morning, Audrey's mother came into her bedroom. "Wake up," she told her daughter. "It's war."

In the early days of the war Audrey did not leave school or stop dancing. Then, one day, the Germans sent everybody out of the town. Outside, in the country, there was very little food. Audrey and her family had to dig vegetables in the winter from the hard ground. When the war finished, Audrey was very thin and weak. People from the United Nations★ came to Arnhem and gave the children milk, sugar, and chocolate. Audrey never forgot them.

★ United Nations: Most countries are in the United Nations. They meet in New York and talk about the world's problems. They try to stop wars.

Chapter 2   A Little Sun in her Eyes

Audrey and her mother moved to Amsterdam after the war. Her mother became a cook. She was not rich, but she paid for Audrey's dancing lessons. Audrey had the best dancing teacher in Holland. Then, when she was seventeen, she had a small part in a travel movie. The director loved her happy face. He said, "A little sun is shining in her eyes."

In 1948 Audrey and her mother moved to London. Her mother worked in a flower store. Friends gave them some money, and Audrey went to the Ballet Rambert. This was the most important ballet school in London. Audrey worked hard at her dancing. She had no time for boyfriends. But one day the ballet school told her, "I'm sorry, but you'll never be a famous dancer. You're too tall."

Audrey was sad, but then something happened. It changed her life. Somebody remembered her from the ballet school, and gave her a small part in a big London musical. Three thousand girls tried to get the part, but the producers wanted Audrey. She quickly found jobs in other musicals. Everybody liked this thin girl with the pretty face and wide smile. "I was not a great dancer," Audrey remembered later. "I threw up my arms and smiled. That's all."

When Audrey was twenty, her photo was in many magazines. She had small parts in three cheap movies, and she was a cigarette-girl in the famous movie, *The Lavender Hill Mob* (1951).

One evening she went to a party and met a rich Englishman. James Hanson fell in love with Audrey. He wanted to marry her and take her to his home in the north of England. Audrey loved him too. He was strong and rich, and she felt safe with him. But there was one big problem: she wanted to be in movies and the theater too. "I don't want to get married now," she told him. "Let's wait."

In 1951 Audrey had a small part in the movie *Monte Carlo Baby*, so she went to the south of France. The famous French writer, Colette, was in the south of France too. She wanted to find a girl for the Broadway* musical of her book, *Gigi*. When she saw Audrey, with her thin arms and legs, long dark hair, and big pretty eyes, she said, "She is Gigi! Half-woman, half-boy. Wonderful!"

Audrey was excited, but nervous. "I can't do that," she told the great writer. "I'm a dancer, not an actor." But Colette did not listen. She called New York and said, "Stop looking for Gigi. She is here!"

Chapter 3   *Roman Holiday*

Audrey was wonderful in *Gigi*, but she did not get too excited. "After *Gigi*, I'm going to marry James Hanson," she told the newspapers. But then something happened, and James had to wait again.

A Hollywood movie producer remembered Audrey from one of her early English movies. He wanted her to be a princess in a big new movie, *Roman Holiday*. Audrey could not say no.

After she finished *Gigi*, she flew to Rome. The most important actor in the movie was Gregory Peck, and Audrey was nervous. This was her first big movie, and Gregory Peck was world-famous. "Maybe he won't like me," she thought. But she was wrong. He was nice to her, and helped her. It was the hottest summer in Rome for years, and the work was not easy. But Audrey was happy and friendly with the other actors. Everybody liked her.

Roman Holiday opened in London on August 20, 1953. In the

* Broadway: a famous street in New York with a lot of important theaters.

Roman Holiday *was Audrey's first big movie, and Gregory Peck was world-famous.*

movie Audrey is a princess, but she does not wear expensive clothes or eat in expensive restaurants. She wants to see Rome and eat ice-cream in the street. She wants to be the same as the other young girls in Rome. The movie made Audrey world-famous. Young girls everywhere wanted to dress in the same way as her.

Now she wanted to be in movies all the time. She was not ready to be James Hanson's wife. James was sad, but he understood. They stayed friends.

Chapter 4   The Right Man

Audrey's next movie was *Sabrina*. Hubert de Givenchy of Paris made her clothes. "A woman does not wear a dress," he told her. "She lives in it." He became her friend for life.

There were two very famous actors in *Sabrina*, William Holden and Humphrey Bogart. Holden liked Audrey very much. Bogart did not like Holden, so he was unfriendly to Audrey too. "Don't be sad. Nobody likes Bogart," Holden told her. "He's unfriendly to everybody." Holden fell in love with Audrey. He wanted to leave his wife and marry her. "She was the love of my life," he said later.

Audrey liked Holden too, but he was not the right man for her. He drank too much and he had a wife and three children. She did not want to hurt his family. But there was something more important than this. He could not have more children, and children were very important to Audrey. When she married, she wanted to be a mother too.

Later in the same year, Audrey went to a party in London and met the right man. He was eleven years older than her, but to her he was wonderful. He was an actor, writer, producer, and director. He knew everybody in Hollywood. He was a good friend of

"A woman does not wear a dress," Givenchy told Audrey.
"She lives in it."

Gregory Peck. He was intelligent, and he could speak many languages. He had a warm and friendly face. His name was Mel Ferrer.

Chapter 5   At the Top

In September 1953, there was a photo of Audrey on the front of *Time* magazine. "She shines with fire in her beautiful eyes," the magazine wrote. The world was in love with Audrey Hepburn, but Audrey was only in love with one man. She wanted to be with Mel Ferrer all the time. He produced a play for her on Broadway, *Ondine*, and she acted in it with him for six months. People liked *Ondine*, and Audrey acted beautifully.

She won an Oscar★ for Best Actress in *Roman Holiday*. Three days later she won a Tony★ for Best Actress in *Ondine*.

These were exciting times for Audrey, but she was very tired. She had to have a vacation, so she flew to Switzerland.

She loved Switzerland. She felt safe there, away from the people and noise of the big cities. She could see white mountains from her windows. Maybe she remembered more than twenty years before—a little girl in her father's arms with lights as white as snow above her head?

Chapter 6   A Good Wife

On September 25, 1954, she married Mel Ferrer in Switzerland. She became pregnant and stopped making movies. Sadly, she lost the baby. She was very unhappy, but Mel was strong. He loved her and was very nice to her.

★ Oscar/Tony: Every year Hollywood gives Oscars to the best movie actors. Tonys are for plays and theater actors.

Audrey acted with her husband in War and Peace *(1955).*

After that, she wanted to be in movies with her husband. She acted with him in *War and Peace* (1955). Then she made *Funny Face* (1956) with the famous dancer Fred Astaire. Mel was not in this movie, but he was near her in Paris. Audrey enjoyed dancing with Fred Astaire. It was a happy musical with beautiful clothes by Givenchy.

In 1956 Audrey made another movie in Paris—*Love in the Afternoon*, with Gary Cooper. This time Mel could not be near her. He was in the United States, so he sent her a new "friend": a little dog. Audrey loved the dog. She took him everywhere and gave him the name "Mr. Famous."

The next year, 1957, Audrey did not make any movies. Mel worked in Spain and Mexico, and Audrey went with him. She cooked for him and helped him with his work. A lot of people in Hollywood were angry with Mel and did not like him. To them

Then Audrey made Funny Face *(1956) with the famous dancer*
Fred Astaire.

he was her boss, more than her husband. They wanted more
movies with Audrey in them.

But Audrey was happy—it was, maybe, the happiest time of her
married life. She had no telephone. She was away from everybody,
and near Mel. This was important to her. "Because next year," she
thought, "I'm going to work in Africa without him."

Chapter 7 "I won't be stupid again"

Audrey went to Africa in January 1958 with her dog and began
work on *The Nun's Story*. It was very different from her other
movies. There was no love story, no music, there were no funny
conversations—and no Givenchy clothes.

In the movie Audrey was a nun, Sister Luke, and she had to wear nun's clothes. The camera could only see her mouth and eyes, but she was more than a pretty face. She was a great actress too, and people loved her.

But great actresses sometimes make mistakes. When Audrey came back to the United States, she was a bird-girl in *Green Mansions*. It was her worst movie. People laughed at it, and this made Audrey sad. She was sad because she made the movie for love. Mel was the director and he never directed a Hollywood movie again.

This was a bad time for Audrey. After *Green Mansions*, she became pregnant again. Mel wanted her to stay at home, but she went to Mexico. In the middle of the movie, *The Unforgiven*, she had an accident. She fell off a horse, and lost her baby for the second time. Mel was nice to her, and Audrey felt very bad. "I'm sorry," she said to him. "I won't be stupid again."

Audrey was a bird-girl in Green Mansions.

Some time later, Alfred Hitchcock, the famous director, wanted Audrey to be in his next movie—a big, expensive Hollywood movie. He sent her the story, and she read it.

"What do you think?" Hitchcock asked. "Will you do it?"

"I'm sorry," Audrey told him. "I don't like the story. It's not for me."

Hitchcock was very angry with her. He made a different cheap, black and white movie with no world-famous actors. "This will be a bad movie," he thought angrily. "It will lose money, and I'll never speak to Audrey Hepburn again." He was wrong about his new movie. Its name was *Psycho*. But he was right about the second thing—he never spoke to Audrey again.

Audrey did not think about Hitchcock very much. She was happy because she was pregnant again. "I won't be stupid this time," she thought. Hollywood wanted her to be in a new musical, *West Side Story*, but she stayed quietly in Switzerland. She did not want to lose a third baby. In January 1960 Audrey had a baby boy, Sean.

After Sean was born, Audrey stayed at home with him. She was happy in Switzerland, with her baby son and her little dog. In the day she went for long walks in the snow. In the evening she sat by the fire and read. Then one evening she read a story by Truman Capote. Its name was *Breakfast at Tiffany's*.

Chapter 8 *Breakfast at Tiffany's*

Audrey wanted to do the movie, but she was nervous about the story. She usually played nice girls—princesses, dancers, nuns— but the girl in *Breakfast at Tiffany's* is not nice. She leaves her husband and goes to New York. She is friendly with bad people. Audrey was also nervous because Truman Capote did not really want her in the movie. He wanted Marilyn Monroe. "Maybe the part isn't right for me," she thought.

Audrey made Breakfast at Tiffany's *in New York and it came to the movie theaters in 1961.*

The director, Blake Edwards, visited Audrey in Switzerland. "It *is* the right part for you," he told her. "You're one of the five biggest actresses in the world. You can do anything. It's time to do something different and dangerous. Yes, Holly's a bad girl. But behind her expensive clothes and dark glasses, she's only a child."

Audrey made *Breakfast at Tiffany's* in New York and it came to the movie theaters in 1961. "She's a European princess; she can't act the part of a poor American horse doctor's wife," some people said. But most people liked the movie very much. In her dark glasses and Givenchy clothes, Audrey was beautiful, crazy, and funny. And they loved her when she sadly sang *Moon River* at her bedroom window.

Chapter 9   Sad Times

Audrey began to have problems after *Breakfast at Tiffany's*. Mel was not happy. "Audrey's becoming more and more famous," he thought. "Maybe she doesn't love me."

Audrey had other problems too. She was a schoolteacher in *The Loudest Whisper* with Shirley MacLaine, but the movie was not successful. It was boring, people thought. One day her dog, Mr. Famous, ran into the road. A car hit him and he died. Then in 1962 she made a very bad movie, *Paris When it Sizzles*. William Holden was also in the movie. He fell in love with Audrey in *Sabrina*, and he was in love with her ten years later. He could not forget her, and he drank. In the evenings, Audrey often went to dinner with her old friend Givenchy. She told him about Mr. Famous and her problems with William Holden.

"But there's something worse than that," she said sadly. "Things are not good with Mel and me."

After *Paris When it Sizzles*, Audrey became happier. She made *Charade* with Cary Grant, and this was a better movie. It was

After Paris When it Sizzles, *Audrey became happier. She made* Charade.

beautiful and intelligent, funny, and exciting. "Maybe," she thought, "the bad times are at an end."

One day, in the winter of 1962, Audrey was at home in Switzerland with her two-year-old son. Suddenly she heard the telephone. Audrey answered it. "Are you sitting down?" somebody said from Hollywood. "You are going to be Eliza Doolittle in *My Fair Lady*!"

Chapter 10 *My Fair Lady*

My Fair Lady opened on Broadway in 1956. Rex Harrison was Higgins and Julie Andrews was Eliza Doolittle. It became the most successful theater musical of all time. Everybody wanted to see the same actors in the movie, but Jack Warner, the producer, had other ideas. He was happy with Rex Harrison, but he wanted a more famous actress for Eliza. He wanted Audrey Hepburn.

In the beginning, Rex Harrison was very unfriendly to Audrey because Julie Andrews was not in the movie. He was also unhappy about money. "Why are you paying Audrey $1,000,000?" he asked the producers angrily. "My part is more important, but you're only paying me $250,000!" Audrey found an answer to this problem. She bought Rex a red bike and they became good friends.

But she could not buy red bikes for everybody. The newspapers also wanted to see Julie Andrews in the movie. Audrey felt sorry for Julie. "But what can I do?" she thought. "The producers want me, and I really want to be Eliza. I can't say no."

Work began in August 1963, and it was not an easy time for Audrey. She had to have singing lessons because she could not sing as well as Julie Andrews. One day, the director said, "I'm sorry Audrey. We'll have to use a different singer." After this, she was difficult with everybody. She shouted at Mel when he visited

She was beautiful in her white hats and dresses.

her. Everybody on the movie heard their fights. Sometimes, in front of the cameras, she started to cry.

My Fair Lady came to the movie theaters in October 1964. The newspapers did not like Audrey's acting in the first half of the movie, but they liked her more in the second half. She was beautiful in her white hats and dresses. And when Professor Higgins hurt her, she acted wonderfully. You could really feel it when she was angry!

My Fair Lady won eight Oscars, but Audrey did not win one. Hollywood felt sorry for Julie Andrews, and gave her the Oscar for her part in the Disney musical *Mary Poppins*.

Chapter 11   A Family Home

Audrey left Hollywood as quickly as possible. She wanted to be near Mel, so she moved to Spain with him for eight months. She wanted to be happy again and to stop fighting. She remembered when she was a child. Her father left her when she was six years old. Now her son, Sean, was the same age, and she did not want him to lose his father.

She then bought a house in a small town in the French part of Switzerland. She had white English flowers in the yard, and Sean played with the other children. For a short time, in 1965, Audrey and Mel were happy again.

Audrey made a successful movie with Peter O'Toole, *How to Steal a Million*. After that movie, young women everywhere wore the same big white sunglasses and short white skirts.

In 1966 she made *Two for the Road*. This was a movie about the problems of married life. Audrey was very good in this movie, but it was more successful in Europe than in the United States. The most important actor in the movie was Albert Finney. He was

Audrey made a successful movie with Peter O'Toole, How to Steal a Million.

younger than Audrey, and she liked him very much. She went drinking and dancing with him in the evening, and had a wonderful time.

In 1967 things started to go wrong again. She made *Wait until Dark*, and people liked it. But Audrey was not happy. She was away from her son, and Mel was friendly with other women.

She became pregnant again, but lost the child. This was the end for her and Mel. "I was very sad when Mel left," she said later. "I was more famous than him, and he felt bad. But I really tried to be a good wife. My family was always more important to me than my movies."

Chapter 12   Married Again

In 1969 Audrey married an Italian doctor, Andrea Dotti. He was ten years younger than her, and he knew her movies.

Audrey lived a quiet life in Switzerland and Rome. She had a baby boy, Luca, in 1970, and became interested in her husband's work. She was most interested in children with problems. "I don't want to make more movies," she told newspapers. "I'm happy as a good wife and mother."

She only made one movie in eleven years: *Robin and Marian* (1975) with Sean Connery. She made it quickly in Spain, when her children were on summer vacation. It was good, but not very successful. Younger people were not interested in a love story between two older people.

Then Audrey heard about her husband's girlfriends, and she

Audrey only made one movie in eleven years: Robin and Marian *(1975) with Sean Connery.*

was very angry. Other women said, "It's not a problem. He loves you. All husbands have girlfriends." But Audrey did not listen to them. "When you love somebody, you have to love them all your life," she said to friends. She left Dotti in 1979.

Chapter 13   A Beautiful New Angel

Audrey only made two or three more movies, and they were not very good. She made them for the money. When she became older, she wanted to do something more important with her life. She remembered her early years, at the end of the war, when she was poor and hungry. Now *she* wanted to help poor and hungry children too.

She started to work for the United Nations. With her new friend, Robert Wolders, she visited the poorest and most dangerous countries in the world. The world-famous actress in Givenchy clothes now worked with hungry children in Africa. She stayed in small towns with no water, and visited sick children in dirty old hospitals. When she was at home, she talked on television about her work.

She had a small part in one more movie: she was an angel in Steven Spielberg's *Always*. Audrey's last words in the movie are, "Do things for others."

In 1992 she traveled to Africa for the last time. When she came back, she was very sick. She got better for a short time and her old friends Elizabeth Taylor and Gregory Peck visited her. But then she became very sick again, and the doctors could not help her. She left hospital and went back to her house in Switzerland. She wanted to see the snow on the mountains again before she died. There were white flowers everywhere inside the house. Her friend Givenchy sent them from Paris. Audrey had one last, quiet Christmas with her family. Before they carried her upstairs to

*The world-famous actress in Givenchy clothes now worked with
hungry children in Africa.*

bed, she looked at everybody. "This was the best Christmas of my life," she said.

On January 20, 1993, Audrey Hepburn died. She was sixty-four. Mel Ferrer and Andrea Dotti came to the church near her house and said goodbye. Elizabeth Taylor said, "God has a beautiful new angel now."

The ground outside the church was white with snow and flowers.

ACTIVITIES

Chapters 1–5

Before you read

1 Do you know any Audrey Hepburn movies? What parts did she usually play?

2 Look at the photos on pages 5 and 7. Who are the people with Audrey? Why are they famous?

3 Look at the Word List at the back of the book. Which are words
   a for women? **b** about movies? **c** about the theater?

While you read

4 What happened first? And then? Write the numbers 1–10.
   a She won an Oscar for best actress.   .....
   b She had a small part as a cigarette-girl in a movie.   .....
   c She met a famous French writer.   .....
   d She played the part of a princess in a big movie.   .....
   e She studied ballet in London.   .....
   f She acted in the musical, *Gigi*.   .....
   g Audrey dug food from the ground.   .....
   h She acted in a movie with Humphrey Bogart.   .....
   i She fell in love for the first time.   .....
   j She acted in a play with Mel Ferrer.   .....

After you read

5 Audrey traveled to a lot of places. Why did she go to:
   a Holland?   **d** Rome?
   b the south of France?   **e** Switzerland?
   c New York?

6 How did these people feel about Audrey, and why?
   a James Hanson   **d** Humphrey Bogart
   b Colette   **e** Hubert de Givenchy
   c William Holden

7 Have this conversation with another student.
   Student A: You are James Hanson. You want Audrey to stop acting and marry you. Tell her about your plans.
   Student B: You are Audrey. You love James but you don't want to stop acting. Tell him.

Chapters 6–9

Before you read

8 Talk about these questions.
    a Will Audrey enjoy life with a husband? Why (not)?
    b Look at the photos from four different movies on pages 10, 11, 13, and 15. Which movie is the most famous? Which movie was not successful? What do you think?

While you read

9 Are these sentences right (✓) or wrong (✗)?
    a Audrey married in Switzerland.   .....
    b Audrey acted with her husband in *War and Peace* and *Love in the Afternoon*.   .....
    c Everybody in Hollywood liked Audrey's husband.   .....
    d Audrey did not make any movies in 1957 because she was sick.   .....
    e Audrey went to Africa without her husband.   .....
    f Audrey lost a baby while she was making *Green Mansions*.   .....
    g Alfred Hitchcock directed Audrey in a movie.   .....
    h Audrey had a child.   .....
    i Audrey sang *Moon River* in *West Side Story*.   .....
    j Audrey became more successful than her husband.   .....

After you read

10 In which movies did Audrey
    a act with her husband?   **f** have an accident?
    b act with Gary Cooper?   **g** play a bad girl?
    c dance with Fred Astaire?   **h** play a schoolteacher?
    d play a nun in Africa?   **i** act with William Holden?
    e play a bird-girl?   **j** act with Cary Grant?

11 Did people like the movies in Activity 10? Why (not)? Does the book tell us?

12 How did these people feel, and why?
    a Audrey, when she made *Love in the Afternoon*
    b people in Hollywood, when Audrey went to Spain and Mexico with her husband
    c Audrey, in 1957

d Audrey and her husband, after they made *Green Mansions*

e Audrey, after she made *The Unforgiven*

f Alfred Hitchcock, after he spoke to Audrey about his new movie

g Audrey, in January 1960

h Audrey, before she made *Breakfast at Tiffany's*

i Truman Capote, when Audrey got the part in *Breakfast at Tiffany's*

j Audrey, in 1962

Chapters 10–13

Before you read

13 Look at the photos on pages 17, 19, 20, and 22. How did Audrey's life change in the last part of her story? What do you think?

While you read

14 Underline the right answers.

a Audrey *sang / did not sing* the songs in *My Fair Lady*.

b Audrey *won / did not win* an Oscar for *My Fair Lady*.

c *Two for the Road* was more successful in *Europe / the United States*.

d Audrey's second husband *worked / did not work* in the movies.

e In the 1970s, Audrey became more interested in *movies / family life*.

f In the 1980s, Audrey worked *in a hospital / for the United Nations*.

g Audrey's last movie was *Robin and Marian / Always*.

h Audrey died in *Africa / Switzerland*.

After you read

15 How were these people important in the last part of Audrey's story?

a Julie Andrews

b Rex Harrison

c Jack Warner

d Peter O'Toole

e Albert Finney

f Andrea Dotti

g Sean Connery

h Robert Wolders

i Steven Spielberg

j Elizabeth Taylor

16 Who said or thought these things? Why?

    a "My part is more important, but you're only paying me $250,000!"

    b "I can't say no."

    c "We'll have to use a different singer."

    d "I was more famous than him, and he felt bad."

    e "It's not a problem. He loves you."

    f "Do things for others."

    g "This was the best Christmas of my life."

    h "God has a beautiful new angel now."

17 Work with another student. You and your friend play a game in a movie magazine and you win three Audrey Hepburn movies. Which movies would you like? Why?

Writing

18 You are Audrey in Spain in 1965. Write a letter to Givenchy. Tell him your feelings about *My Fair Lady*, the Oscars, and Mel. What are your plans? Why?

19 How and why were these important to Audrey?

    a Mr. Famous   **b** children   **c** the color white

20 You are Mel Ferrer. Write about your life with Audrey for a movie magazine. What were your happiest times, and what were your saddest? Was Audrey a good wife and mother? Why (not)? Why did you leave her?

21 In 1970, Audrey thought, "I don't want to make more movies. I want to be a good wife and mother." You are a movie producer. You think that Audrey is making a big mistake. Write her a letter.

22 Write a letter to a movie actor. Ask for a photo.

23 Write about Audrey life for a newspaper on the day after she died.

WORD LIST *with example sentences*

act (n) She *acted* in three movies last year. She is a great *actress*.

angel (n) There are pictures of *angels* on the walls of the church.

ballet (n) I learned *ballet* for years, but I can't dance well now.

baroness (n) Mrs. Thatcher was *Baroness* Thatcher for the last years of her life.

become (v) When you *become* a doctor, will you work in a hospital?

dig (v) I *am digging* in the backyard because I want to put more trees there.

direct (v) Did George Lucas *direct* the *Star Wars* movies?

musical (n) *Mary Poppins* was a book, then a movie, and now you can see the *musical* at the theater.

nervous (adj) He is always *nervous* before he gives a talk to schoolchildren.

nun (n) She was a *nun*, so she never married.

part (n) Brad Pitt played a small *part* in *Thelma and Louise*.
Which *part* of the country are you from?

play (n) We read *Hamlet* last year, and we are going to read another *play* this year.

poor (adj) She comes from a *poor* family, but now she is very rich.

pregnant (adj) She is *pregnant* with her third child.

princess (n) *Princess* Diana died in a car accident in 1997.

produce (v) She *produced* the movie, so she had to find the money for it.

safe (adj) We felt *safe* when the airplane was on the ground again.

successful (adj) He is a very *successful* writer and makes a lot of money.

travel (n/v) I enjoy *travel*, but I really like to be at home.

war (n) They fought in the *war* between the north of the country and the south.